Intuitive WISDOM

4880 Lower Valley Road, Atglen, PA 19310

For Alex and Ian,
the world is a better place
with the two of you in it.

Belief consists in accepting the affirmations of the soul; unbelief, in denying them.

—Ralph Waldo Emerson

CONTENTS

GETTING TO KNOW YOUR TAROT DECK 5

The Major Arcana
Getting to Know the Major Arcana and Card Meanings 6

0 Fool 8	11 Justice 20
1 Magician 9	12 Hanged Man 21
2 High Priestess 10	13 Death 22
3 Empress 11	14 Temperance 23
4 Emperor 12	15 Devil 24
5 Hierophant 13	16 Tower 25
6 Lovers 14	17 Star 26
7 Chariot 15	18 Moon 27
8 Strength 16	19 Sun 28
9 Hermit 18	20 Judgment 29
10 Wheel of Fortune ... 19	21 The World 30

The Court Cards
Level of Power 33
Actual Person in Your Life 34
Getting to Know the Court Cards 35
Reversed Court Cards 36

The Pentacles Court
King of Pentacles 37
Queen of Pentacles 37
Knight of Pentacles .38
Page of Pentacles 39

The Wands Court
King of Wands 40
Queen of Wands 40
Knight of Wands 41
Page of Wands 42

The Cups Court
King of Cups 43
Queen of Cups 43
Knight of Cups 44
Page of Cups 45

The Swords Court
King of Swords 46
Queen of Swords 46
Knight of Swords 47
Page of Swords 48

The Minor Arcana

Getting to Know the Minor Arcana..................49

THE PENTACLES SUIT

- Ace of Pentacles 51
- 2 of Pentacles 52
- 3 of Pentacles 53
- 4 of Pentacles 54
- 5 of Pentacles 55
- 6 of Pentacles 56
- 7 of Pentacles 57
- 8 of Pentacles 58
- 9 of Pentacles 59
- 10 of Pentacles 60

THE CUPS SUIT

- Ace of Cups 73
- 2 of Cups 74
- 3 of Cups 75
- 4 of Cups 76
- 5 of Cups 77
- 6 of Cups 78
- 7 of Cups 79
- 8 of Cups 80
- 9 of Cups 81
- 10 of Cups 82

THE WANDS SUIT

- Ace of Wands 62
- 2 of Wands 63
- 3 of Wands 64
- 4 of Wands 65
- 5 of Wands 66
- 6 of Wands 67
- 7 of Wands 68
- 8 of Wands 69
- 9 of Wands 70
- 10 of Wands 71

THE SWORDS SUIT

- Ace of Swords 84
- 2 of Swords 85
- 3 of Swords 86
- 4 of Swords 87
- 5 of Swords 88
- 6 of Swords 89
- 7 of Swords 90
- 8 of Swords 91
- 9 of Swords 92
- 10 of Swords 93

PUTTING IT ALL TOGETHER: The Cross Tarot Spread 94

- How to Phrase Your Questions 94
- Reading Your Cards 95
- The Cross Spread 96

YES OR NO ANSWERS 96

GETTING TO KNOW YOUR TAROT DECK

A Tarot deck longs to be played with! Although regarded as a mystical and sacred artifact by many, Tarot is actually a practical system of image-based wisdom that speaks to our subconscious to reveal the truths we have forgotten how to see.

Composed of 78 cards, each with a title and illustration, there are three parts to a traditional Tarot deck:

- 22 Major Arcana cards
- 16 Court cards
- 40 Minor Arcana cards

The Major Arcana

The 22 Major Arcana cards in a Tarot deck guide us through with the grander order of existence: large-scale external forces impacting our lives, universal archetypes, and the distinct stages of the ultimate journey of the soul. Let's embark upon the journey through the transcendent Major Arcana together—the 22 quintessential stages for the evolution of the individuated human spirit.

GETTING TO KNOW THE MAJOR ARCANA AND CARD MEANINGS

Remove the Major Arcana cards from the deck. Shuffle and fan the 22 cards in front of you. Close your eyes, quiet your mind, and focus upon the following question:

"What must I face in order to see more clearly?"

With your left hand, choose the Major Arcana card that answers this question, and place it upright before you. Now, follow these steps:

1. Meditate upon the images on the card: What do you see? What do they mean to you? How do they make you feel? Are you blocking this card's energy from your life in any way? Or, conversely, are you immersing yourself in the card's energy to the point of excess? Does this card remind you of anyone? What is your relationship to this person? Is there any closure that is still necessary for you in this relationship? Does this card remind you of an experience or a dream?

2. Next, look up the meaning of this card and read it thoroughly from the Major Arcana chapter. Sit in a comfortable position for a few minutes and consider the meaning of the card. Compare your instinctive responses to the written ones.

3. Finally, reread this card's part in the Hero's Journey. Enter a prayerful, meditative state with the card either in front of you or in your hands, and open yourself to embrace its energy. If it scares you, face this fear. If you have trauma associated with its images, look at the memories thoroughly, and your bothersome feelings associated with it will begin to dissipate. If you view this energy as either "good" or "bad," look at the entire energy as it is, rather than putting labels or judgments upon it.

It is a good idea to eventually do this with each of the Major Arcana cards. One suggestion with regard to meditation: the goal of meditation is to get beyond your mind and body. If you struggle with meditation, it is either because your body wants control or your mind does. If your body wants control, you will feel a need to scratch or move constantly. If your mind wants control, you will either find your mind tends to drift into tangents or else you might create grand mental structures around the images rather than simply looking at them and seeing what is there. In order for meditation to succeed, you must use your spiritual eyes rather than your physical or mental ones.

0 Fool
THE UNPREDICTABLE

Upright Meaning:

- Infinite possibility
- Childlike wonder, innocence, and discovery
- A new beginning or spiritual journey
- Folly, eccentricity, even mania
- Unexpected events or natural disasters
- Need for caution—watch out!

Something you don't expect is coming. The Fool always cautions us to be careful—the unexpected and uncontrollable is entering our lives, possibly on a worldwide scale. Something in your life will be dissolving or disintegrating, but this is not necessarily a bad thing. The Fool can also represent a child in your life, places or things beyond your reach, and natural events. We humans are so domesticated by our routines, so used to feeling in control of our lives, however unhappy we are in them. The Fool tells us to leave our comfort zone and embark into the wild unknown.

Reversed Meaning:
You feel trapped, either fearful of things you cannot control or else out of control of yourself. Your inner world is chaotic, wild, and volatile. You want drastic change. You may also be concerned about a child or world events that are out of your control. You seek more control, excitement, risks, distraction, and drama to compensate for your unstable inner world. Stop fixating upon your problems and what you lack, and instead focus upon dismantling the lies and stories you tell yourself to justify your suffering by opening yourself up to all the ecstatic possibilities of existence. You must be willing to take that first step off the cliff to transform your life.

1 Magician

KNOWLEDGE IS POWER

Upright Meaning:

- The will and power to act
- Communications and messages
- Intellect, learning, and the mind
- Adaptable, easily influenced
- Craftiness, cunning, manipulation

At its most basic level, this card warns that you need to listen carefully to the message of the reading, for it contains crucial information for your life. The situation calls for using your head rather than your heart—be logical, rational, and objective in the situation. Knowledge is power, and there is substantial power available to you, but beware of behind-the-scenes manipulation or counterintentions. You are easily swayed right now and prone to inconsistency. There is an important message or communication coming, so be ready and listen up! The Magician can also foretell an upcoming short trip or vacation.

Reversed Meaning:
You are justifying and rationalizing your actions. You are confused and waffling back and forth with regard to the subject at hand: you know you do not know and need wisdom. Be honest with yourself and seek a trustworthy authority outside yourself for sound advice.

2 High Priestess
MYSTERIES TO BE UNVEILED

Upright Meaning:

- Journey within to discover the truth
- Regeneration and manifestation
- Receptive power of intuition
- Women, cycles, and changes
- Mysterious, moody, hidden

The High Priestess unveils what is significant. She is always a powerful influence in a reading and never to be taken lightly, for she reveals the "verb," the action, the direction of the reading. At its most basic level, an upright High Priestess says that you are in your prime or at the height of your powers with regard to the subject under consideration. In a woman's reading, this card can suggest issues with menstruation and feminine cycles. In a man's reading, this card can indicate a young woman in your life. The Priestess reveals your emotional world and always points toward the most essential portion of the reading: if surrounded by cards of a positive nature, the High Priestess communicates that now is the time to act; if surrounded by negative cards, she warns that now is not the time. The High Priestess portends the start of something—generally the birth of a goal and sometimes even the actual birth of a child.

Reversed Meaning:
The High Priestess rules our emotions and subconscious: she helps us bring forth what is deep inside us so that it might be resolved. You have lots of potential growth with regard to the subject at hand. You are moody and overemotional, longing to give birth to something new but struggling to manifest the creation. Look deeply within yourself for your own answers: this is a time of introspection, a time to prepare and gestate, rather than to act.

3 Empress
GREAT MOTHER

Upright Meaning:

- Feminine power and sexuality
- The fullness and pleasures of womanhood
- Power of love
- Motherhood and Mother Nature
- Abundance and prosperity
- Beauty, fruitfulness, art, luxury

The Empress is a beautiful card, literally; she beautifies and sweetens the surrounding cards and situation whenever she shows up in a reading. In a man's reading, she can represent his mother or lover as well as suggest a potential lover entering his life. In a woman's reading, this card suggests that you are a wonderful woman and mother; the Empress can also indicate that you are fertile and able to become pregnant (or perhaps are already so). The Empress promises improvement in money matters. In a reading regarding love, this card brings feminine romance and seduction in contrast to the more masculine raw, animal passion. If next to cards of a negative nature, this card may indicate dissipation, vanity, and waste.

Reversed Meaning:
You long to experience the full blessings of womanhood. If surrounded by mostly positive cards, you are ready and able to embrace love and healing right now. If next to cards of a more negative nature, you feel alone and long for the lover or child you never had, or mourn your relationship with your mother (or your relationship with your children as a mother); you feel empty, ugly, sexually frustrated, stifled by your own mother and the natural way of things. In a man's reading, this card may indicate his worry about or longing for a woman in his life or concerns about being a good provider. You must learn to nurture yourself first before you can nurture others.

4 Emperor
ALL FATHER

Upright Meaning:

- Masculine power and authority
- Fatherhood
- New beginnings and taking risks
- War, conquest, competition, and conflict

The Emperor announces that something new is beginning in your life, as well as discusses anything happening to you right now. The Emperor suggests a powerful, aggressive authority figure, whether it is you yourself or a person in your life depends upon the position of this card in the Tarot spread. It often indicates your father; in a man's reading it may discuss you as a father, or in a woman's reading it may discuss the father of your children. If you are involved in a conflict and the Emperor appears upright in your reading, you will be victorious. When neighboring positive cards in a reading, the Emperor advises you to take the risk and go for it—you will be successful. If this card is surrounded by negative cards, on the other hand, it can warn of an angry, potentially violent man in your life, as well as general problems with power and authority.

Reversed Meaning:
The reversed Emperor addresses who and what you really are, once all the facades and intentions are stripped away; the surrounding cards often reveal what you need to focus upon in order to return to yourself. You may want to become a father, be worried about your father, or be concerned about your children and your children's father. You desperately desire to start something new, conquer something, or take a new position of leadership. If next to negative cards, you feel angry and trapped in a civilized life that subdues but never truly satisfies you.

5 Hierophant
TRADITION AND SECURITY

Upright Meaning:

- Following the traditions set forth by religion, culture, and schooling
- Professional reputation and standing in society
- Successful financial endeavors; increase in resources and prosperity
- Love of indulgence and possessions

At the basic level, the Hierophant speaks of security and those things that serve as our foundation—physical, financial, and emotional resources. This card points toward the control that societal standards exert over us. When well placed, it suggests successful financial endeavors and an increase in resources and prosperity; however, when the card is poorly placed, there will be problems with resources or the current financial difficulties will continue. An upright Hierophant may advise you that it's time to seek an expert's advice (such as a lawyer, psychologist, doctor, or financial consultant) in the area under consideration. As your Significator, this indicates you are at the top of your field and have a worthy professional reputation: You are or will soon be quite successful in your career. When well placed, this card can indicate winning a lawsuit. If poorly placed, this card often warns that you are stuck in the monotony of day-to-day survival, weighed down by the obligations of pleasing those in authority.

Reversed Meaning:
In order to establish stability, you are turning toward external authority figures (teachers, clergy, experts, politicians) to prescribe how you must live rather than trusting yourself, willingly abiding by the standards and restrictions of culture, education, religion, economics, and patriotism in order to be "right" or "good." The Hierophant reversed often suggests that you are worried about resources and are trying to make more money;

perhaps you are even considering consulting a professional about a particular area of concern. Watch out for resisting a necessary change in your life out of your own insecurity. You enjoy the finer things in life and tend to fall apart at the first sign of financial trouble.

6 Lovers
ATTRACTION AND CHOICE

Upright Meaning:

- Appearance, image
- Romantic love
- Infatuation—falling in love with the reflection of yourself you see in the other
- Superficial, short-term concerns and commitments
- Making a difficult choice

At the initial level, the Lovers discusses the appearance of the matter, your image, or the world's surface perception of you. It can refer to a communication that has occurred or needs to occur. In a question of romance, the Lovers indicates a passionate, all-consuming infatuation that will not last long—for each is in love with the image of the beloved and the beauty felt in their union, rather than an awareness of the true self of the other. The Lovers generally indicates a short duration of the matter at hand, no longer than 12 to 18 months. If poorly placed, this card can suggest difficulty in making a crucial choice between options that seem the same.

Reversed Meaning:

The love you feel is exciting and intoxicating, but beware of becoming lost in your infatuation or, even worse, becoming obsessed. You are concerned about your image and looks to the detriment of your health and the truth. You might be seeking greater depth of insight into a particular contract or communication but lack more than a superficial understanding of the matter. If neighboring negative cards, the Lovers reversed may warn of your preoccupation with the condition of your skin, from acne to wrinkles. Focus on finding long-term solutions rather than the current short-term solace you are seeking.

7 Chariot
THE FOUNDATION

Upright Meaning:

- Confront the contradictions and the truth of your life as it is right now
- Take up the reins of your own life and command of your destiny
- Your roots, home, foundation, family, children
- The natural and unavoidable conclusion of the matter

When the Chariot is upright in a reading, it reveals the foundation of the matter under consideration: what's really beneath it as well as its natural and unavoidable conclusion. This card also reveals the way to get control of a situation. The Chariot speaks of your roots, home, children, and beginnings; it may also refer to your more nurturing parent. This card reminds us of what is out of our control, and instructs us to get control: although we don't choose our start in life, it is our choices that shape and mold how we experience our life and where we end up.

Reversed Meaning:

You are struggling with the reality of your life's circumstances and the possibility of something ending before you are ready. If the card is well placed, you are seeking effective avenues of control and working well within the confines of the situation. If surrounded by negative cards, you are moody, oversensitive, and complaining rather than taking responsibility for your part in your circumstances.

8 Strength
TAMING THE BEAST

Upright Meaning:

- Confront and tame one's body, the animal nature
- Lust, passion, vitality, self-esteem, ego
- Happiness, fun, amusement, luck
- Love of life (or the lack thereof if poorly placed)

Strength rules our general health and physical vitality as well as the things that make life worth living for most of us—happiness, fun, and amusement. If surrounded by positive cards, Strength suggests you will be lucky in the endeavor at hand. An upright Strength card discusses your general health, vitality, and love of life. It often reveals that you are involved in a love affair of a sexual nature or else portends the opportunity for one. If poorly placed, Strength reveals your poor health, low self-esteem, and general lack of passion and life force.

Reversed Meaning:

Life has lost its flavor: you feel exhausted, outside yourself, and bored with the repetitive cycles of simply existing. You may be seeking a new sexual partner. Thwarted in your attempts to attain your initial goals, you are beginning to withdraw and give up the chase. It is time to reconnect with your center and befriend your ills—stop viewing them as obstacles that must be overcome, and instead recognize them as lessons that must be learned. Remember your passions and pursue them as a knight pursues his love in order to reawaken your hunger for life.

NOTE:

In the earliest known Tarot decks, the Major Arcana had no numbers, but generally, earliest Tarot decks placed the Strength card as 11 and Justice as 8. The Rider-Waite Deck broke with this tradition and reordered the Strength card as 8 and the Justice card as 11 to better correspond to each card's astrological correlation. Crowley changed them back to their original placement in his famous Thoth Deck. Many see the placement of the cards as interchangeable today, while others hold quite an opinion upon where the cards are to be placed in sequence.

9 Hermit

THE WORK OF WITHDRAWAL

Upright Meaning:

- Analyze the details of the situation
- Turn within to find the truth you seek
- Seclusion, asceticism, pilgrimage
- If poorly placed—restriction, fixation, obsession

The Hermit warns us to pay attention to the particulars. Analyze the situation. Work out the details. The Hermit may also discuss illness. This card may signify someone you have consulted (or will consult) for advice, or else discuss the value of the advice that you have received; whether for good or ill depends upon surrounding cards. If well placed, the Hermit can say that you are denying the physical pleasures of life and ascetically "going within" to progress spiritually.

Reversed Meaning:
Beware of being stuck in a fixation. When the Hermit is reversed, it often reveals your worries about illness or the details of a situation: you feel alone and isolated. There is also a longing for perfection that motivates higher mental pursuits. If surrounded by negative cards, you are worried about your job or lost in the endless mental loops of your mind. Still your mind. Stop all the criticisms and the judgments. The answers you seek will be found only in integration and wholeness, not in endless overanalysis and asceticism.

10 Wheel of Fortune
ABUNDANCE AND EXCESS

Upright Meaning:
- Luck, prosperity, and general increase
- Spiritual blessings; your destiny as opposed to your future
- Pride, preoccupation with material possessions, and grandeur
- The winner in any matter

The Wheel of Fortune returns us to our divine source, to our destiny, to truth. It always speaks of expansion, growth, progression, blessings, and spirituality; perhaps you are entering a phase of growth and learning or are focused on spiritual pursuits. Your concerns will be alleviated, and a period of prosperity is at hand. When placed positively, the Wheel signifies vast expansion of blessings in your life; when poorly placed, however, it warns of excess and its painful consequences: problems with obesity, intoxication, pride, or material obsession. The Wheel can also discuss a judgment in your life; whether in the courtroom, by the clergy, or through life's circumstances depends upon surrounding cards. When positively placed, this card signifies the winner in the subject under discussion.

Reversed Meaning:
You feel like the great Wheel of Fortune is turning your life upside down, again, and you're tired of the ups and downs it brings—learning to receive these changes, without criticism or complaint, is the road to finding your bliss. You long for prosperity, blessings, and spiritual growth yet struggle with obsessing over your deficiencies and shortcomings. It is time to unstick the parts of your life that have become stagnant and unchanging, releasing their energy potential through action and movement. Guilt and resentment only justify your inaction: abundant life comes from a life lived abundantly!

11 Justice

PARTNERSHIPS AND OPPOSITION

Upright Meaning:

- Partnerships
- Justice and adjustment
- Contracts and lawsuits
- Open enemies and opposing forces

The Justice card reveals the truth about your partnerships: to know whether it refers to a business or personal partner, look at the surrounding cards. If cards of a negative nature surround the Justice card, there will be serious troubles with partnerships and open enemies. When poorly placed, Justice can often suggest the ending of a current partnership. On the other hand, when well placed, Justice blesses an existing partnership or even announces a new beneficial alliance on the horizon. Justice upright can also discuss your contracts or lawsuits; look to surrounding cards to know if you will win or lose.

Reversed Meaning:

You are internally imbalanced. Justice reversed reveals your worries or longings about partnerships; perhaps you are worried about a partner or else desire to begin a new partnership. Make the necessary adjustments to your lifestyle and your choices to find the symmetry that you lack.

12 Hanged Man
VISIONS AND DELUSIONS

Upright Meaning:

- Mystic, visionary
- New perspective
- Self-sacrifice or deception
- Dreams and our subconscious

The Hanged Man turns our world upside down. Just as the Hanged Man looks at the world from an upside-down position, this card encourages us to be imaginative and consider new vantage points (perhaps even those that we deem to be "fiction"). If surrounded by positive cards, this card signifies the power of redeeming love over self-sacrifice: choosing to enter the darkness of the unknown in order to find the light of awareness. However, the Hanged Man generally says you are lost in a fog, caught in delusion. Your head is in the clouds, and you are either hiding or missing something. The Hanged Man can also suggest that someone is going to trick or "pull the wool" over your eyes.

Reversed Meaning:
Proceed carefully! You are consumed with worries about what you don't know and are lost in your own ideals of how things should be, unable to live in the real world and perhaps even sacrificing yourself needlessly. You may be deceiving or deluding yourself. Only if the card is extremely well placed, pursue your madcap ideas for yourself and humanity and don't worry about the naysayers: genius is never appreciated in its own time.

13 Death
CHANGE AND TRANSITIONS

Upright Meaning:

- Change and endings
- Transition
- Loss, grieving, letting go
- Debt or bills due

Change of a life-altering nature is imminent in your life; something is ending so that something else may begin. If poorly placed, the Death card warns of problems with bills, taxes, and debt . . . possibly even a bankruptcy. If well placed, it can speak of an inheritance or successfully overcoming credit problems. Your suffering is necessary: transition can be painful, but when we break out of the rigidity of our dead past decisions and choices, the next stage of our awakening begins.

Reversed Meaning:
You are living in a changed reality but have yet to embrace your new existence. You wish to destroy or change something; you long for transformation. Perhaps you are struggling with deep safety and survival issues, or else you seek power and control. If the card is poorly placed, you may be consumed with the fear of dying or conversely about your mounting debt, and if the card is very poorly placed, you could be suicidal. Your emotional responses are more about you and your feelings of loss than about the reality of your situation: you need to grieve, let go, and move on.

14 Temperance
THE ART OF ALCHEMY

Upright Meaning:

- Moderation in all things
- Alchemical merging of opposites to attain transformation
- Long-term goals, higher education, spiritual quests
- Beware of going too far, too fast, and of risk taking

Temperance is moderation or self-restraint, but to "temper" is also to reform a substance by reheating and then cooling it. This card deals with the art of merging opposites to form a new and better you. Temperance often suggests you are going too far and need to chill out or "temper" your current actions; otherwise you'll crash and burn. It also speaks of your goals and ambitions, as well as the methods you are using to attain them. If you are considering a long trip, now is the time to take it. Temperance encourages you to pursue further education, higher philosophies, or deeper spirituality.

Reversed Meaning:
You feel inspired to realize a long-standing aspiration and do whatever it takes to bring it into reality. Continue pursuing your aims but consider the risks and beware of burnout. Rest and recuperation are essential for you right now.

15 Devil
PAYING YOUR DUES

Upright Meaning:

- Reap what you sow
- Reputation
- Profession and career
- Reveling in the pleasures and treasures of carnality

At the heart of the Devil card is exalting physicality to the detriment of spirituality, and paying dues for what we have done. The Devil commands you to get control of the situation, for a great material force or temptation is propelling you out of control and into chaos. It may also discuss your career or reputation. Upright, it often represents a boss or authority in your life; with regard to a court case, it represents the judge and the judge's decision. If well placed, it says you are focused, climbing to the top of the situation at hand with hard work, or that your life is settled and under control. If poorly placed, the Devil may suggest trouble with career or reputation and painful consequences as a result of poor choices. When neighboring positive cards, the Devil encourages us to get in contact with the sensual pleasures of having a physical body.

Reversed Meaning:
Materiality and having the things of this world matter much more to you than eternity or authenticity. When reversed, the Devil says that you are worried about and focused upon your career and standing in the world. Perhaps you are actively working to progress up the corporate ladder, or else you are concerned about problems with an authority figure or boss. You are unhappy about paying the consequences for your past actions or inactions.

16 Tower

THE DESTROYER

Upright Meaning:

- Lightning flash of truth
- Destroyed foundations
- Shattered forms, perceptions, and lies
- Attack, bloodshed, battle

The Tower upright brings some sort of unavoidable purifying destruction into your life. It is up to you whether this shatters you or makes you stronger. Conflict and war are imminent. Well placed, and this destruction will ultimately be for the best. Poorly placed, the Tower warns of ruin and possible danger in the matter under consideration. The Tower upright occasionally speaks of an older woman in your life.

Reversed Meaning:
Look to the cards that surround the Tower reversed to discover where you invest your energy and action, what impassions and angers you, as well as the direction of your drive and zeal: it reveals that for which you burn. You are deeply concerned about survival on all levels right now: look to surrounding cards for hints on how to redirect your focus. If the card is poorly placed, uncontrollable anger is bubbling up from inside you right now, making you lose control and quite possibly becoming a danger to yourself and others.

17 Star

THAT WHICH FREES US

Upright Meaning:
- Dreams and ideals
- Humanity at its best
- Future, friendship, possibility
- Hope and help for difficult times

In a reading, the Star tells us of our future, our dreams, and that which can free us from our current situation. The Star generally portends a favorable future for you and may point to unexpected help from a friend, large group of people, or the public. People will impress you, and possibilities will be realized when the Star card is drawn. However, if poorly placed, the Star can sometimes point toward dreaminess and deceived hope. When surrounded by a preponderance of negative cards, the Star may also warn about an impending fall (literal or figurative) in your life, for it is our biggest dreams that have the potential to fall the farthest.

Reversed Meaning:
You are seeking a dream or an ideal, something to free you from your current situation. If the card is poorly placed, your dreams may be trapped within you, but you have no idea how to manifest them in the external world and bring them about. If the card is very poorly placed, you are deceiving yourself into believing you know what is best for the situation and everyone involved, even to the detriment of others and the facts.

18 Moon

DARK NIGHT OF THE SOUL

Upright Meaning:

- Breakthrough
- Restriction and obscurity
- Hidden scandals and horrors
- That which scares us
- Artistic genius, psychicism

The Moon is the gateway to our unconscious mind, those horrors that we imagine things to be, rather than their reality. It is our desire to avoid what scares us, those things that we don't wish to be aware of or to see fully. The Moon upright warns that you are not seeing something important: some truth is hidden in the matter under consideration. Something is restricting you. To know what is hidden or restrictive, look to the surrounding cards. Perhaps you are caught up in a religion of abdication, have an enemy you are unaware of, or else are unaware of a family scandal or love affair that has been hidden from you. If well placed, the Moon upright can suggest that you have considerable psychic abilities and are able to see what others cannot.

Reversed Meaning:
You are facing a crisis of faith or a "dark night of the soul." You fear facing the truth, want to avoid confronting the darkness, and have suppressed negative memories or moments in order to avoid experiencing the pain associated with them. You are hiding something important from those around you or from yourself. You may even be anxious about being trapped, arrested, or imprisoned in some way. Don't give up; on the other side of this lowest point, you will find the illumination you seek.

19 Sun

LIGHT TO DISPEL THE DARKNESS

Upright Meaning:

- Happiness, gain, joy, and riches
- Spiritual enlightenment
- Increase in health and vitality
- Innate talents and abilities
- Personal flair and style
- Youthful, vigorous, and cheerful

The Sun is always positive if well placed. Usually, this card suggests glory, gain, riches, and general health and vitality for you. The Sun shines light on the matter under consideration, illuminating the way through. This card may also represent a benevolent leader in your life, your father, or a person you idolize or admire. Your finances will improve, your health will get better, your mood will lift, and you will find that which you seek.

Reversed Meaning:

You are "seeking the light"; whether it is through immersion into the process of enlightenment and illumination, happiness and passion, or self-esteem and self-understanding depends upon the surrounding cards. When well placed, the Sun says that you are either generally healthy or else focused upon improving your health. If very poorly placed, the Sun can suggest arrogance, melodrama, and vanity on your part, as though you think you are the center of the universe.

20 Judgment
RESURRECTION

Upright Meaning:
- Verdict or determination
- Resurrecting the past
- Forgiveness, surrender, acceptance
- Humanity's long-term outcomes

Judgment is the purifying fire that burns away all the refuse in order to bring the truth to light; it exerts tremendous pressure on the coal of our lives (and on humanity as a whole) to transform us into the diamond we're meant to be. When you pull this card, it indicates you've been placed within the crucible of fire—will you be consumed, or will the trial transform the canvas of your life into the precious gem or priceless art you have the potential to become? This card cautions that this is a serious situation: you are about to make a large blunder. Pay attention, this is critical. An enormous change is imminent; it will be painful, but it will destroy your self-made rubbish. This card reveals the final judgment or determination of a matter, without appeal in the material plane. The Judgment card may also warn you that someone is "playing with the dark" or hiding something in the situation and can't be trusted. Now is the time to be careful, be honest, and forgive your former mistakes to embrace your new life.

Reversed Meaning:
Indicates the hell that you are willing to go through to achieve heaven: your struggles to transform yourself and humanity. You are struggling with accepting a permanent in your life or the life of a loved one. If the card is poorly placed, you may also be struggling with secret compulsions and acting outside morality or ethics: what is happening inside you is so consuming that you cannot trust yourself (and neither can anyone else).

21 The World

MASTERY

Upright Meaning:
- Full circle
- Completion and perfection
- Integration and synthesis
- Mastery by merging with All
- World events, duty, limitation

The World card represents world events and the interconnection of the physical universe: this card points to the crux of the matter under consideration and the synthesis of all the elements involved. If very well placed, this card suggests that you have reached mastery in a particular area, and so it is time to return to the rest of the world and share your gift(s) with those in need. When well placed, the World upright in a reading suggests that you are doing your duty—whatever you are attempting, it will all come together and work out. The World can also suggest that external events or world events are going to have a profound impact in your life. If surrounded by cards of a negative nature, there may be a conflict with an older man or a government agency. The World, when poorly placed, might also indicate that you are avoiding doing what is appropriate in the situation. The World reveals the weight of the matter, what is so important to you that you can't see what to do in the situation because you cannot see past the weight of the significance you've attached to it.

Reversed Meaning:

Generally, the World reversed tells you that you need to be more dutiful! You may fear aging or are resisting a limit placed upon you. Set in your ways, your inflexibility and unwillingness to bend are weighing you down so much that you aren't free to react objectively in response.

If the card is poorly placed, you are rebelling against society and the establishment, refusing to separate your own significances from the truth of the matter. If the card is well placed, you desire to share your gifts with the world.

> ### NOTE:
>
> Some Tarot deck creators change the names of their Major Arcana cards. For example, Crowley's alterations are well known and often copied: Magician to the Magus, Justice to Adjustment, Wheel of Fortune shortened to Fortune, Strength to Lust, Temperance to Art, Judgment to the Aeon, and World to the Universe. Even if a card has a different name, however, the basic meaning of the card remains the same.
>
>

THE COURT CARDS

While the 22 Major Arcana cards in a Tarot deck deal with the grander order of existence, the Minor Arcana cards focus on the daily events, people, and experiences of living. In addition to the Major Arcana, the remaining 56 cards of a Tarot deck are divided into four sets of 14 cards:

10 Minor Arcana with four Court cards—each set of 14 cards attributed to a particular "suit":

PENTACLES (sometimes called Coins or Disks)
WANDS (also named Staves, Staffs, or Rods)
CUPS
SWORDS

There are four Court cards in each suit:
KING, QUEEN, KNIGHT (some decks rename him Prince), and
PAGE (other common names are Knave or Princess)

Just as the Major Arcana represent the 22 powers that are generally beyond the world of men, so the Court cards represent the powers that rule the world of men.

NOTE:

Some Tarot decks call their Court cards by unique monikers. To consider Kings, for example, Aleister Crowley's *Thoth Deck* changes Kings to Knights, and I've seen sundry other titles for the King such as Father, Speaker, Master, or Mentor.

Many people new to Tarot find the Court cards the most difficult to interpret in a reading, but the following guidelines will help you understand these noble lords and ladies and their messages for you as they appear in a Tarot spread. There are two basic ways to interpret a Court card:

- Level of Power
- Actual Person in Your Life

LEVEL OF POWER

The Level of Power tells you the amount of energy available to accomplish what you wish:

- Kings, just like their medieval counterparts, have substantial power and complete support. They portend enduring strength that is wholly supported to accomplish all goals. A King usually predicts *great success in the endeavor under discussion*.

- Queens, while they have access to the same power as their husbands the Kings, resort to more-hidden, indirect methods in their wielding of it. A Queen in a reading has formidable power, but for some reason the energy is trapped, bubbling beneath the surface, waiting to give birth or manifest an undertaking. Queens often communicate a *need to remain dormant in a given situation: it is prudent to wait instead of act*.

- Knights, as soldiers of action, have the far-greater passion and virility of youth that is lacked by their elders, without the earned wisdom of experience and the resources of the King and Queen. In a Tarot reading, a Knight indicates that any venture must be completed quickly because Knights *accomplish their tasks alone, with little support from others. Their power does not endure. Knights are great for starting projects, but not for completing them*.

- A Page in medieval society was generally the younger child of a nobleman who either served as a knight's attendant or else was a royal messenger at court; thus, although Pages have little or no power in the present, there is hope for their future prospects. When a Page appears in a Tarot reading, *there's not enough behind the issue to carry it to fruition in its current stage of development. It's not worth the effort*.

ACTUAL PERSON IN YOUR LIFE

Look for the following if you suspect the Court card represents an actual person in your life:

- A Page represents a child or youth.
- Knights are young adults, generally single—a person who is actively seeking, but hasn't yet attained, a complete sense of self.
- A Queen is generally a woman who is older than you or any mother.
- A King suggests an older man who has attained some measure of success or self-knowledge, or any father.

Each person displays the characteristics of the corresponding suit. Each of these suits is attributed one of the four classical elements (or states of matter) of the physical universe:

- Wands are attributed to Fire (plasma) and matters of creativity, desire, and power.
- Swords are attributed to Air (gas) and the domain of the mind, communication, and discord.
- Cups are attributed to Water (liquid) and the inner realms of emotion, intuition, and love.
- Pentacles are attributed to Earth (solid) and the material resources (usually career and money) to attain one's goals.

NOTE:

Occasionally, decks exchange the attributions of Wands and Swords, making Swords correlate to Fire and Wands correlate to Air.

GETTING TO KNOW THE COURT CARDS

For this spread, separate the sixteen Court cards and shuffle them thoroughly. Now, choose the Court card that you instinctively feel best represents you in this present moment. If you choose a King, take out the other three Kings and lay all four of them upright before you. If you choose a Queen, lay the four Queens before you; if you choose a Knight or a Page, do the same, so that you end up with four cards in front of you. It is time to look at the faces that you show the world or personas with which you mask yourself, as well as look at the deeper truth behind each of these masks. Follow these three steps during your consideration:

Similarities and Differences: Look at the images upon each of the cards. How are these characters the same? How are they different? Reread the information about each one in the Court card chapter. Consider which card most attracts you. Why? Which most repels you and why? What can you learn about yourself by comparing and contrasting these four cards with yourself?

Stage of Life: Next, consider the stage of life, level of power, and phase of progression that is represented by the four characters. Do you like the phase that is represented by these cards? Why or why not? In which areas in your life are you currently acting out this stage of life? In which areas in your life are you currently acting out this level of power? In which areas in your life are you currently acting out this phase of progression? What do you need to do to embrace the energies that you perceive in these cards; what do you need to let go of? Does this card define the real you, or only the persona or mask you show the world?

People in Your Life: Now spread out all 16 Court cards in front of you. Consider the people in your life today and assign each to the Court card that best represents them. What can you learn about these people in your life based upon their Court card? Who are the people and Court cards with whom you wish to surround yourself? Who are the people and Court cards from whom you would prefer to distance yourself? Can you gain any deeper insights about the people in your life and your relationship with them when you consider the Court card that you associate with them?

REVERSED COURT CARDS

If a Court card is reversed, it does not represent an actual person in your life but instead either characterizes the energy that emanates from you or else suggests that you are thinking of or concerned about a person that the Court card characterizes.

THE PENTACLES COURT

KING OF PENTACLES

Upright Meaning:

- Prosperous professional man
- Commanding, authoritarian
- Decent, honorable, hardworking, stable
- Strong power and support to succeed

Reversed Meaning:
You are either concerned about or seeking a man who exhibits the qualities of the King of Pentacles (such as an expert in a particular profession), or else wish to grow in the areas in which the King of Pentacles excels: finances, career, reputation, and success in the material realm. If the card is poorly placed, you need to be more dedicated and dutiful in order to achieve your goals, or else you think you are considerably more successful than you really are.

QUEEN OF PENTACLES

Upright Meaning:

- Successful businesswoman
- Self-contained, pragmatic, commonsense
- Inspires integrity in others
- Wait to act—now is not the time

Reversed Meaning:
You are either concerned about or seeking a woman who exhibits the qualities of the Queen of Pentacles, or else wish to grow in the areas in which the Queen of Pentacles excels: finances, career, reputation, and success in the material realm. If the card is poorly placed, you may be too passive or too careful in the matter under consideration. Beware of helping others in such a way that they refuse to help themselves: abundance comes from within, not from being enabled.

KNIGHT OF PENTACLES

Upright Meaning:

- Dedicated to service and sacrifice
- Focused on details and routine
- Methodical, critical, efficient
- Great beginnings but little follow-through

Reversed Meaning:
You are either concerned about or seeking a young man (or a pet) who exhibits the qualities of the Prince of Pentacles, or else wish to grow in the areas in which the Prince of Pentacles excels: attention to details and meticulousness in material matters. If the card is poorly placed, you are being too critical and need to gain some perspective. Break out of your routine and mix it up.

PAGE OF PENTACLES

Upright Meaning:

- Loves food and fun and is generally jolly
- Enchanting youth enchanted with life
- Enjoys the finer things in life and spending money
- Plans will not work out

Reversed Meaning:

You are either concerned about or seeking a person who exhibits the qualities of the Page of Pentacles, or else are struggling with problems similar to those of the Page of Pentacles: perhaps you feel insecure or else have lost hope that you will succeed with money or career. If the card is poorly placed, you may be behaving too childlike or immature and need to grow up before the harsher realities of life force the issue.

THE WAND COURT

KING OF WANDS

Upright Meaning:

- Heroic conqueror
- Daring, uplifting, exciting
- Powerful, adventurous, risk-taker
- Strong power and support to succeed

Reversed Meaning:

You are either concerned about or seeking a man who exhibits the qualities of the King of Wands, or else wish to grow in the areas in which the King of Wands excels: creativity, passion, and power. Perhaps you desire to start something new; if the card is poorly placed, you are wrestling with anger issues. Curtail your temper and your tendency to rush into things.

QUEEN OF WANDS

Upright Meaning:

- The quintessential artist
- Inspiring, vibrant, creative
- Passionate and willful
- Wait to act—now is not the time

Reversed Meaning:
You are either concerned about or seeking a woman who exhibits the qualities of the Queen of Wands, or else wish to grow in the areas in which the Queen of Wands excels: creativity, passion, and accomplishment. Perhaps you feel you've lost your passion and spark. If the card is poorly placed, you are being too passive or too careful in the matter under consideration.

KNIGHT OF WANDS

Upright Meaning:

- Carefree, playful, impulsive young man
- Eternal optimist and freedom loving
- Philosopher, rebel, gambler
- Wonderful ideas but little follow-through

Reversed Meaning:
You are either concerned about or seeking a young man who exhibits the qualities of the Prince of Wands, or else wish to grow in the areas in which the Prince of Wands excels: optimism, confidence, and personal growth. If the card is poorly placed, your happy-go-lucky and devil-may-care attitude is getting you into trouble.

PAGE OF WANDS

Upright Meaning:

- Creative, precocious, endearing youth
- Needs to be the center of attention; lively entertainer
- People pleasing (sometimes manipulative) and pleasure seeking
- Goals will not be realized

Reversed Meaning:

You are either concerned about or seeking a person who exhibits the qualities of the Page of Wands, or else are struggling with problems similar to those of the Page of Wands. If the card is poorly placed, you are fixated on seeking pleasure or else feel creatively stagnant or powerless. You want to be noticed, seeking acknowledgment and recognition.

THE CUPS COURT

KING OF CUPS

Upright Meaning:
- Counselor and protector
- Affectionate, emotionally supportive, generous
- Fatherly, spiritual, intuitive
- Strong power and support to succeed

Reversed Meaning:
You are either concerned about or seeking a man who exhibits the qualities of the King of Cups, or else wish to grow in the areas in which the King of Cups excels: emotion, intuition, love, and spirituality. Perhaps you want to see a psychologist, long for a family, or desire to purchase a new home. You tend to give too much in your desire to help.

QUEEN OF CUPS

Upright Meaning:
- Fiercely maternal
- Empathetic, loving, nurturing
- Reflective, sentimental, insightful
- Wait to act—now is not the time

Reversed Meaning:

You are either concerned about or seeking a woman who exhibits the qualities of the Queen of Cups, or else wish to grow in the areas in which the Queen of Cups excels: emotion, intuition, love, and spirituality. If the card is poorly placed, you may be too passive or too careful in the matter under consideration; on the other hand, you might have latent psychic abilities that are starting to surface. Loving by nature, you long to mother something—you may crave to literally become a mother, or else you might wish to give birth to a project.

KNIGHT OF CUPS

Upright Meaning:

- Young unmarried man in love with the idea of love
- Charming, romantic, poetic
- Tragic hero
- Means well but generally unable to deliver on his sweet promises

Reversed Meaning:

You are either concerned about or seeking a young man who exhibits the qualities of the Prince of Cups, or else wish to grow in the areas in which the Prince of Cups excels: romance, imagination, and empathy. Perhaps you desire to woo a new love or else want to take up a spiritual pursuit. You feel like you are constantly putting on a performance for those around you. A charming, loving, adaptable person, you are too

easily influenced by your environment and those around you. You are exhausted but cannot seem to find any real rest. You feel drained because you are trying to keep everyone else satisfied. Focus on your own abundance—love will wait.

PAGE OF CUPS

Upright Meaning:

- Youthful elation, angst, and sexuality
- Avoidance of pain to the detriment of development
- Juvenile, willful, secretive
- Cravings will remain unsatisfied

Reversed Meaning:
You may be worried about the erratic and secretive behavior of a young person in your life who behaves like a Page of Cups, or else may feel sexually repressed and overemotional yourself. Beware of hiding in secrets and dodging paying your debts in the attempt to avoid pain at all costs. If the card is poorly placed, you are fervently focused on the limitations of another, all the while desperately hiding the truth of your own lack. You need to admit your childishness and take responsibility for yourself if things are to improve.

THE SWORDS COURT

KING OF SWORDS

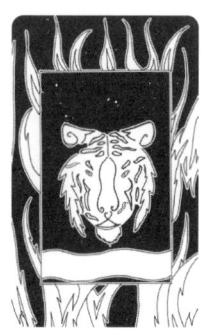

Upright Meaning:

- Sage, mentor, advocate
- Ethical and rational
- Objective, just, noble
- Strong power and support to succeed

Reversed Meaning:

You are either concerned about or seeking a man who exhibits the qualities of the King of Swords, or else wish to grow in the areas in which the King of Swords excels: knowledge, wisdom, communication, and reconciliation. You may be worried about matters of partnership.

QUEEN OF SWORDS

Upright Meaning:

- Mature, independent woman
- Intelligent, ruthless, demanding
- Martyr who broods behind your back
- Wait to act—now is not the time

Reversed Meaning:

You are either concerned about or seeking a woman who exhibits the qualities of the Queen of Swords, or else wish to grow in the areas in which the Queen of Swords excels: intelligence, communication, and discord. Perhaps you want something to end or fear something ending, such as a marriage or a job. You need to figure out what you really want: you have those around you dancing in response to your masterful handling, but by not making a decision you are only hurting those involved (including yourself) and prolonging the inevitable. Get out of your head and feel what's happening around you.

KNIGHT OF SWORDS

Upright Meaning:

- Clever young man
- Ingenious, adaptable, mercurial
- Talkative, opinionated, comic
- Uncanny ideas that disappear just as quickly

Reversed Meaning:

You are either concerned about or seeking a young man who exhibits the qualities of the Prince of Swords, or else wish to grow in the areas in which the Prince of Swords excels: cleverness, adaptability, and the ability to see the similarities and relationships between things. Perhaps you want to return to school or are concerned about the proper credentials or paperwork to accomplish your goals. If poorly placed, this card suggests that you are looking only at the superficial, surface details of the issue. Shut up and listen—you might learn something.

PAGE OF SWORDS

Upright Meaning:

- Freethinker and freedom loving
- Restless, inquisitive, idealistic
- Different to the point of being weird
- Idealistic to the point of impracticality

Reversed Meaning:

You are either concerned about or seeking a person who exhibits the qualities of the Page of Swords, or else are struggling with problems similar to those of the Page of Swords: perhaps you feel lost and without purpose. You might be upset over feelings of not fitting in, while at the same time not feeling free. Perhaps you are waiting for someone to save you from your current situation or from your own poor choices. Admit you are dramatizing your own significance, and stop acting the victim: only you can save yourself.

The Minor Arcana

GETTING TO KNOW THE MINOR ARCANA

Separate the 40 Minor Arcana cards into four piles according to each suit, in order from Ace to Ten. Put them in front of you in four rows of ten, with the Aces to the far left and above each other, the Twos to the right of the Aces and above each other, and so on. Consider the elemental themes of each suit. Do you see any consistencies or lessons that you might learn from the progression and conclusion of a particular suit? Conversely, do you see any consistencies or lessons that you might learn from a particular set of numbers (the Aces, the Twos, etc.)? Now choose one card from each suit that best represents where you are in your own life today with regard to each suit's theme. Is this where you wish to be? What needs to be changed? What pitfalls need to be avoided? What does this say about you and your own journey through this life?

THE PENTACLES SUIT
the symbol

The Pentacles suit represents the receptive Earth element. A pentacle is the symbol of a pentagram (five-pointed star) engraved within a perfect circle or a coin. Earliest Tarot decks use a coin for this suit, and it was not until the late 1780s that Comte de Mellet changed the suit from coins to pantacles (meaning talismans), which Eliphas Levi and other ceremonial magicians later reworked into pentacles. Some people are bothered by the image of a pentagram, conditioned to misunderstand it as "satanic" or "evil" in some way when pictured upside down, much as modern Western society now views the swastika—an ancient solar symbol of light in mythology—as the twisted symbol of Nazism. Each of the elements is represented by the four lower points of the pentagram—from right to left, the points represent water, fire, earth, then air—with the upper point representing spirit, which (ideally) remains senior to the other elements. An upside-down pentagram suggests the perversion of this natural order.

    The pentacle, however, is an upright five-pointed star with a circle around it. Traditionally, circles are a symbol of eternity, for they have no beginning and no end; the circle is also a symbol of the cyclical nature of existence. Circles simultaneously contain and protect. The pentacle is a beautiful visual symbol of a spirit incarnated or "embodied" into the physical universe.

Ace of Pentacles
POWER OF EARTH

Key Concepts:

- Success in finances, career, or physical happiness
- Now is the time to begin
- Establish a safe and secure foundation for yourself

Upright Meaning:
The promise of success in any material endeavor is at hand, whether in finances, career, or physical happiness: now is the time to begin. This card can also warn you to protect yourself in the physical realm.

Reversed Meaning:
You have within yourself all the desire, possibilities, and power necessary for success, but they lie dormant within you, unable or unwilling to manifest as of yet. Your attention is captured by the possibility of solid accomplishment and manifesting your aims in the physical universe.

2 of Pentacles
SUCCESSFUL CHANGE

Key Concepts:

- Successful change in the material realm
- Career and finances improve
- You will win (even if you don't deserve it)
- Triumph for the body at the expense of the spirit

Upright Meaning:
Successful change in the material realm, but to the detriment of spiritual progression. Career and finances will improve. If the card is well placed, you will win the court case or the promotion—even though you may not deserve it. If the card is poorly placed, forceful control is required in order to resolve a difficult situation.

Reversed Meaning:
If you do what the surrounding cards demand, then the situation will improve. You tend to be rigidly orthodox, moral, austere, and ambitious to a fault, driven by the desire for prominence. This card in the reversed position indicates that there is a need for you to accept full responsibility for your position and exert control in order for the situation to improve. It may also indicate that you are seeking a harmonious change to the circumstances, but what underlies this wish is a desire to further your own situation. You are using the respect of others to prove your own value to yourself; hence your spirituality rests upon the authority that is granted to you by others.

3 of Pentacles
TRIUMPH AFTER TOIL

Key Concepts:

- Success will come only after very hard work
- Don't give up just because you feel exhausted and inadequate
- Your ideas are good ones, but be prepared to fight for them

Upright Meaning:

Success in the material realm as a result of hard work; opportunities for success are approaching—don't miss them. The work that you are doing or are thinking about having done is worthwhile, but it will not be easy. You will not like the authority's judgment in a case under determination, but it's best for everyone.

Reversed Meaning:

You are driven by the desire for power and authority but are frustrated by the restrictions to your success. You may be lonely at work and burdened by heavy responsibility, perhaps even working with undependable people.

4 of Pentacles
GREED AND ACQUISITION

Key Concepts:
- Rise to the top in career, money, and recognition
- Success breeds greed for greater accomplishment
- Only those who are willing to give will be able to enjoy what they receive

Upright Meaning:
When upright and well placed, this card promises material attainment and power as well as stabilization of finances and career. You may receive special recognition or the assistance of an influential person in some way. If poorly placed, this card suggests that you are (greedily) holding on much too tightly to material possessions—you must *release* the grip for prosperity to flow.

Reversed Meaning:
You are dissatisfied with your current situation and have designs to find or create material wealth. If poorly placed, this card can suggest that you are pretending you have more (or are more) than is actual, indicating excessive spending on your part as though you're wealthier than you actually are. Finally, you may be aiming beyond your reach, using acquisition of resources to prove personal worth.

5 of Pentacles
FINANCIAL TROUBLES

Key Concepts:

- Deal with your money problems now or they will become unmanageable
- Bills go away only if you pay them
- Consult an expert

Upright Meaning:
There are serious problems with credit and bills, but it's still possible to get control of your financial worries . . . perhaps with the help of a specialist? There may be difficulties with lawsuits: if you are currently receiving legal or financial advice, it's flawed. It's time to get control of the use of credit, curtail spending habits, and stop living as though consequences will disappear. Focus on the future, retirement, and insurance matters.

Reversed Meaning:
This card reversed implies that you are attempting the impossible goal of getting what you want without paying the necessary price. You are awash in worry and self-pity as a result of your material troubles yet are resisting all change because of possible failures or "things getting even worse." Deep-seated security issues need to be faced or else you will create your own self-fulfilled prophecies.

6 of Pentacles
PROSPERITY

Key Concepts:

- Great security and luck in financial matters
- Everything will flow your way naturally
- Present and future investments will pay off
- Your children will be okay

Upright Meaning:

Financial resources are flowing your way; current investments (especially of an artistic nature) will have great value in the future, and any hunches regarding profitable new ventures will flourish. This card also reassures you that your children are stable and will succeed.

Reversed Meaning:

If the card is well placed, you are seeking material comforts and are aware of your good fortune. If very poorly placed, a reversed card can suggest that you are overly attached to physical comforts and worrying about unfounded money problems.

7 of Pentacles
DISCONTENT

Key Concepts:

- You don't have the resources (either personal or financial) to finish the job
- Don't sign any contracts right now—you don't have all the facts
- You will run out of resources if you continue
- Sometimes hard work is not enough

Upright Meaning:
Despite considerable hard work, you are in the midst of a difficult period: there are insufficient resources on all levels, from improper nutrition to limited cash. There may be contractual dilemmas, labor disputes, cutbacks, and layoffs. You are even befuddled in selecting partnerships.

Reversed Meaning:
You are simply unsatisfied with the results of your labors and are bogged down by considerable financial commitment. If the card is poorly placed, you may resort to subterfuge in order to alleviate your plight. Despair underlies your actions, and your compensation for personal lack of fulfillment is to compulsively STOP others in their endeavors (especially those who are more content) and make them wrong to somehow justify your own failures.

8 of Pentacles
FIXATION

Key Concepts:

- Fixation on the insignificant to avoid the facts
- Stop obsessing about what's not working and move on
- Current investments won't pay off
- Penny wise but pound foolish

Upright Meaning:

The current matter is not worth pursuing. It's time for you to distance yourself from the current situation and gain a broader perspective with regard to what's troubling you. Whatever you have now invested your energy into—whether a diet, a lawyer, or an investment—will not pay off because you have missed the big picture.

Reversed Meaning:

If very well placed, this card tells you that you need to pay more attention to the details. If the card is poorly placed, you are obsessed with aspects of the situation that don't matter while missing the things that do. Often this card reversed suggests that your attention is stuck on a particular viewpoint as a result of the desperate attempt to prove your own vision of how things should be, rather than seeing what is. You are fixating on the details to avoid seeing the truth.

9 of Pentacles
INOPPORTUNITY

Key Concepts:

- Don't start anything new
- Be careful of ill-timed opportunities
- Be wary of unreliable and enticing partnerships
- You're missing something—be careful

Upright Meaning:
Now is not the time for anything new! A situation or person sweetly entices you, who is lost in misperception: the timing is wrong and the essentials of the circumstance(s) don't add up. You need to be cautious at work, especially with a woman at work; there will be delays and uncertainty on the part of any partners because they're currently unimpressed with you. Wait before making any major decisions or purchases—this is not the time.

Reversed Meaning:
You are entangled in your feelings regarding issues of health, love, and work and therefore are making ill-timed decisions, more consumed with emotions rather than the facts of the matter. This reversed may show an imprudent partnership with a woman. If poorly placed, this card can suggest that you are misperceiving people at work, being judgmental and selective based upon emotional reactions rather than objectivity.

10 of Pentacles
STABLE ACCOMPLISHMENT

Key Concepts:

- Enjoy the fruit of your labors—you've earned it
- The money you need is coming
- This is a good time to move on or up
- Material contentment

Upright Meaning:

This card promises well-deserved job prosperity and wealth. The money that is needed to pay someone else is coming—either from a settlement or else from another unexpected venue. This card may herald a homecoming or moving to a new and better place. If poorly placed, this card suggests that you need to plan ahead, since there is an arduous task necessitating patience and attention to detail before taking action; the slow and steady pace is always preferred when this card comes up.

Reversed Meaning:

If the card is well placed, you are experiencing a state of contented fullness in your life. If the card is poorly placed, you may be actively seeking (or worrying about the loss of) wealth and success. A reversed 10 of Pentacles may simply indicate your talents: writing and teaching, a brilliant analytical mind, and a propensity to garner wealth.

THE WANDS SUIT
the symbol

Conjure the image of Professor Dumbledore from the *Harry Potter* sensation, or else Gandalf from J. R. R. Tolkien's *Lord of the Rings* trilogy. What crucial instrument of power was neither wizard ever without? A long piece of wood that each used to channel his extraordinary powers. The legendary magical wand (or staff) of the mighty mage serves as the symbol for the transmissive Fire element of the Wands suit. Why are wands typically fashioned out of wood? Wood serves as the ideal conductor for the destructive and transformative power of fire. In tales of myth and legend, the magic wand graphically portrays this powerful combination of phallic masculinity with fiery force. Just as the magician masters the art of change in conformity with the will, so the wand is traditionally his (or her) most well-known tool for transformation. Therefore, Wands govern the realms of creativity, desire, and power.

Ace of Wands
POWER OF FIRE

Key Concepts:
- Success in the areas of desire, creativity, and power
- Achievement of goals and creative endeavors
- Long-term plans come to fruition

Upright Meaning:
The Fire element is developing in your life right now, bringing desire, creativity, and ample power. Now is the time for potent, forceful action in order to grasp whatever it is that you wish.

Reversed Meaning:
If the card is well placed, you possess the capacity to succeed in the endeavor(s) under consideration; if the card is poorly placed, you believe that you will succeed, but there are obstacles that must first be acknowledged and faced. To know the obstacles, look to the surrounding cards.

2 of Wands
AGGRESSIVE CONQUEST

Key Concepts:
- Make it happen, take charge, take the plunge—you will triumph
- Wavering and second-guessing will bring failure
- The others will follow you

Upright Meaning:
It's time to "take the bull by the horns." Lead the others into the new enterprise with gusto! What the situation needs is dominating, aggressive force: if you take control and face the unknown head-on, then you will succeed. This card may also forecast a sudden situation or accident coming that will demand spontaneous, forceful action on your part.

Reversed Meaning:
You are competitive, need to be in the lead, and want to do more, more quickly than anyone else. You tend toward belligerence and mow down others in the overwhelming drive to get your own way. Some kind of physical or competitive action is necessary for your well-being.

3 of Wands
ESTABLISHED STRENGTH

Key Concepts:

- You hold power and control in the current situation like a king rules his kingdom
- Leadership is handed to you, so wield it nobly and justly
- Watch out for family or group dissention

Upright Meaning:

Your status in the situation is one of assertive, regal, accomplished power with a hint of arrogance. In a woman's reading, this card may suggest a new love encounter with a sincere, younger man. If the card is poorly placed, there may be a problem with divergent viewpoints within the family, or else a situation that will call for decisive, assertive action on your part in defense of your position.

Reversed Meaning:

You are a strong-willed leader, who hates daily tedium and loves initiating new change. If the card is well placed, you have a lucid vision of what needs to be done and how to do it. If the card is poorly placed, you need to beware of quick action without careful planning, as well as act shrewdly in handling opposing viewpoints that may challenge your leadership.

4 of Wands
APPARENT PERFECTION

Key Concepts:

- Everything seems wonderful, but it's a lie
- You are making poor decisions everywhere—at home, at work, and in love
- Stop treating those around you as obstacles rather than individuals

Upright Meaning:
The situation(s) has the appearance of perfection, without the substance. Nothing is working in its current form: you are at odds with and making poor decisions about your lover, and any current business deals or partnerships have a feeble foundation: the home is a "house of cards." There are probably even problems with the mother-in-law.

Reversed Meaning:
Like the director of your own play, you are responding to other people as the roles that you have assigned to them and critiquing their performance, rather than seeing them for who they actually are. If the card is well placed, you may be a late bloomer in love, are finished with the current relationship, or else have entirely lost the desire to marry. If the card is poorly placed, you are unstable, impetuous, and determined to get what you want—at all costs.

5 of Wands
CONFLICT

Key Concepts:
- Conflicts, disagreement, dissension
- Problems with authority figures and experts
- The show of pride and posturing to cover self-doubt

Upright Meaning:
This card promises conflict between the parties involved. There will be problems with bosses or authority figures. You are burned out and run down: there are problems with blocked vitality, insecurity, and sexual troubles. There will be impassioned differences between older and younger generations, with each side being unwilling to bend because each considers itself to be in the right.

Reversed Meaning:
You are intensely concerned and even depressed about the conflict(s) that consume you right now. Be careful not to be too bold, rash, or insistent that your way is right, unable or unwilling to see the other's point of view. In a man's reading, this card reversed always expresses his basic dissatisfaction with his life, as though in mourning for the lost chances of his youth.

6 of Wands
VICTORY

Key Concepts:
- Success in all endeavors
- You will prevail over your problems
- Even in a really negative reading, this card brightens the outlook

Upright Meaning:

Even if poorly placed, this card promises victory, success, and good luck: no worries. You will succeed in overcoming all dilemmas as well as probably attract some kind of fame, attention, or leadership opportunity.

Reversed Meaning:

You are optimistic, love a good gamble, enjoy children, and take great pride and satisfaction in your life's circumstances—even if a tad excessively. If the card is very poorly placed, you must curtail your tendency to gamble and beware of "blowing your own horn."

7 of Wands
VALIANT RESISTANCE

Key Concepts:
- Many obstacles to overcome
- The harder you push, the harder you will be pushed back
- Watch for loss of credibility, job, or relationship
- Time to quit—it's a lost cause

Upright Meaning:
At face value, you have great strength and will to accomplish your goals, but equally strong external forces are working against you. There may be trouble with credit or love affairs. This card can even discuss a loss of job or lover because of cross-purposes. Attend to a moderate illness or infection resulting from a recent unexpected event, loss, or trauma: it is potentially serious since it affects the basic life force of the body's entire system. Beware of troubles due to reckless seeking of distraction in pleasant sensation. If very well placed, this card commends you for your Herculean effort but still encourages you to give up the lost cause and choose a more reasonable course of action.

Reversed Meaning:
If the card is well placed, you are displaying considerable valor in the face of mounting opposition. If not, you are behaving as a bully, controlled by your impulse for personal gratification, and forcing yourself into an inappropriate relationship or position.

8 of Wands
FLEETING FORCE

Key Concepts:

- Slow down!
- Impetuous seeking of long-term ambitions
- Tendency to rush in and not finish
- Surprise visit from afar

Upright Meaning:
You are missing the vital details of the current situation because of your focus on distant goals and desires. This card advises you to slow down, because you are rushing much too rapidly in all matters. Watch out for speeding tickets, as well as potential problems with paperwork or credentials as a result of not completing the requirements. There may be a temporary visit by a foreigner, a guru, or someone who has been traveling abroad.

Reversed Meaning:
You are acting with an impulsive swiftness that will not endure. You may be planning a long trip, investigating a spiritual philosophy, or even considering studying a foreign language: no matter what it is, you are rushing into it and will not follow through.

9 of Wands
REALIZED POTENTIAL

Key Concepts:

- The potential is yours to realize your aims
- You've done the work and now have the potential to succeed
- A long voyage, significant move, or long-term goal will soon be realized
- Your children will attain their goals

Upright Meaning:

The potential exists for you to accomplish your goals. A long journey, going overseas, or a major move may be in the future. Now is the perfect time to pursue a college degree or follow a spiritual aspiration. This card brings a cause for optimism no matter how negative the surrounding cards.

Reversed Meaning:

If well placed, this card describes you as an imaginative optimist who believes that honesty and ideals are more important than any relationship. If very poorly placed, it suggests that you tend to be dogmatic about your extreme and unorthodox ideas.

10 of Wands
OPPRESSION

Key Concepts:

- Unforeseen anxiety and oppression
- A confrontation is coming with a suppressive person or group
- Stop blaming yourself and move on
- If you don't stop, you could have a nervous breakdown

Upright Meaning:

Beware! This is a time of stress, oppression, and suppression from unexpected sources. There may be a challenging encounter with suppressive philosophies coming, or else a confrontation with an older person who fiercely objects to your current purposes. You are assuming responsibility for situations that are out of your reach.

Reversed Meaning:

You are overwhelmed, are going in too many directions at once, and could suffer a nervous breakdown from sheer overloading of yourself. Beware of hopelessness and let go of what you cannot change: doing too many things poorly is worse than doing nothing at all.

THE CUPS SUIT
the symbol

For most people, the legend of the Holy Grail is either a subject for movie magic—from the comedy *Monty Python and the Holy Grail* to the action-adventure *Indiana Jones and the Last Crusade*—or else a dim memory of Arthurian legend from high school and college literature courses. Tradition has it that King Arthur lost most of his Knights of the Round Table when they embarked upon the Quest for the Grail, fabled to be the very cup from which Jesus drank at the Last Supper and which Joseph of Arimathea later used to catch Christ's blood as he hung on the cross. The Holy Chalice or Grail is a vast and complex symbol of literary, historical, mythological, and spiritual import. This chalice serves as the perfect symbol for the Cups suit, which represents the receptive Water element. Just as Wands and Swords are tall, piercing, prominent phallus-like symbols, so the hollow depths of the Chalice represent the female vagina and womb, waiting to receive the masculine force, which sparks its process of creation through the sacred merging and bliss of sexuality, as the two become one with a greater whole. Cups signify the fertile substance of the universe that unites in order to create, and thus rules issues of emotion, intuition, and love.

Ace of Cups
POWER OF WATER

Key Concepts:

- Success in all emotional endeavors
- Follow your intuition right now
- Heralds a new relationship
- Now is the time for a sacred pilgrimage or rite

Upright Meaning:

The Water element is churning and broiling within you right now, expanding your intuition and emotions. A new relationship (possibly, but not necessarily, romantic) is on the horizon. You may be discovering your inner artist. Now is the time to embark upon a spiritual quest. If poorly placed and if you have asked about a partner, this card suggests that your love interest is a lazy, pleasure-seeking opportunist (all the worst aspects of the Water element).

Reversed Meaning:

You will either be seeking a new relationship or else focusing your energies upon plumbing the emotional depths within. If the card is well placed, you would do well to follow your instincts right now. If the card is poorly placed, you could be caught up in the quagmire of your raging emotions, or else dissipated and full of pretense (the worst aspects of the Water element).

2 of Cups
TRUE LOVE

Key Concepts:

- Harmonious relationships and reconciliation
- You've found true love
- Expansion of family by marriage, birth, or inheritance

Upright Meaning:

In matters of love, this is the real thing. There will be harmonious love and family relationships, possibly a family inheritance or reunion. This card may predict an addition to the family, either by marriage or birth.

Reversed Meaning:

You are either searching for love or else wonder if you have found it. You may desire reconciliation with your spouse, mother, or family.

3 of Cups
ABUNDANCE

Key Concepts:
- You are entering a time of abundance—accept and enjoy it
- Increase in lovers, affection, and pleasure
- If the card is poorly placed, watch out for love affairs and cheating

Upright Meaning:
If the card is well placed, you are experiencing a period of abundance and operating from an attitude of "the more the merrier" right now: you are probably either finding pleasure in multiple relationships rather than in commitment to one person or else are surrounded by multiple romantic opportunities. If poorly placed, this card suggests that you (or someone in your life) is cheating.

Reversed Meaning:
You are either being tempted to cheat on your significant other or else suspect another of cheating. Conversely, you may be consumed with an all-pervasive desire for more. If very well placed, this card can indicate remarkable ingenuity in the realms of speaking and writing on your part. Watch out for boredom giving you an excuse for your excesses right now.

4 of Cups
BLENDED PLEASURE

Key Concepts:

- Blended pleasure as you remain in a less-than-perfect situation
- Dominant feminine influence in your life
- If the card is poorly placed, problems with life cycles and children

Upright Meaning:

It is a time of blended pleasure for you: you will remain in the present situation yet won't be completely satisfied. If the card is poorly placed, there may be troubles with hormones, menstruation, menopause, or children. Because of the basic dominance of the feminine inherent in this card, in a man's reading it may show bisexuality, effeminacy, a lack of sexual balance, or a strong attachment to the mother. Things tend to last at least four years (seeming far too long to you) when this card is drawn.

Reversed Meaning:

If the card is well placed, you demonstrate a high level of emotional maturity, nurturing, self-sacrifice, and awareness of the needs and feelings of others, especially with regard to your children. If poorly placed, this card can show that you are suffering from too much feminine influence and are overly sensitive to the reactions of others. There is an unwillingness to leave home or make any change that might adversely affect another. Beware of resenting your current situation as an excuse for your own inaction.

5 of Cups
HEARTBREAK

Key Concepts:
- Loss of pleasure and desperate avoidance of pain
- Downhill spiral of despair, anger, and regret
- Financial disaster
- Blaming outside circumstances for personal mistakes

Upright Meaning:
This card portends sadness, depression, bankruptcy, financial disaster, personal failures, and emotional distress in an ever-increasing downward spiral. Even if the card is well placed, you are currently or will soon experience a profound loss in pleasure. This calls for severe, controlled action in order to cope with these mounting tribulations.

Reversed Meaning:
If very well placed, this card reveals your inner strength to transform or change a seemingly impossible situation. Normally, however, this card reversed reveals that you are internally awash in anger, depression, pain, and loss. It often suggests that you may be overreacting to a perceived hurt, rather than a real one. You must find a healthy release to your pain by recognizing its true source. Pain is not the problem; it is the avoidance of pain and blaming others and outside circumstances that is the problem. The message of this card is to cease avoiding the discomfort of pain and instead seek its cause, for it is only in facing the cause of our pain that we can discover its cure.

6 of Cups
AFFECTION

Key Concepts:

- Affection and sentiment
- Tendency to give up—DON'T
- Life changes that challenge our security needs
- Difficulty establishing or accepting boundaries

Upright Meaning:

At its surface level, affection is sweet devotion and attachment, often associated with the sentiments of childhood. Affection, however precious it seems in the moment, does not last. At its most basic level, affection is the state of being "affected" by another. When this card is drawn upright, it suggests an exaggerated time of being easily affected by the emotions of those around you and the whims of circumstance—with lots of changes and high moments immediately followed by low ones. If the card is well placed, this affection is poignant and bittersweet. If the card is poorly placed, you feel at the mercy of these affections. There may also be extreme changes in handling other people's money, especially in the realms of debt and taxes, often of a legal nature. This card warns you not to quit prematurely: finish what has been started. This card occasionally heralds a drastic life change.

Reversed Meaning:

Affection is a poor replacement for love. Instead of facing your pain, you are seeking pleasure in sensation to compensate. You exhibit an extreme black-and-white mentality and have trouble setting healthy boundaries or accepting the boundaries set by others. If the card is poorly placed, there may be extremes in sexual behavior, control issues, and power struggles. If the card is well placed, it may be time to heal the emotional baggage from your childhood and single-mindedly seek self-improvement along with the deeper mysteries of life.

7 of Cups
POISONOUS ILLUSIONS

Key Concepts:

- Pretending that minor matters have great significance
- Rivalries, dirty secrets, jealousies, and dangerous partnerships
- Elaborate illusions to avoid painful consequences

Upright Meaning:
This card portends losing oneself in illusion to escape internal emptiness; as the sensations and interactions of the physical universe cease to satisfy you, you begin attributing significance to the dream of satisfaction itself, thereby attempting to artificially craft the emptiness of experience to mean something more. There will be extreme energy imbalances; a poison is invading your life. This card may caution you of a serious infection to be attended to immediately, or else counsel against the overspending of money for frivolity and comfort (perhaps even using another person's credit). There may be heated fights and secrets kept between partners. Watch out for a purely sexual affair of the "fatal attraction" variety. This card may warn of an abusive or suppressive person in your life. If very well placed, this card could indicate an inheritance from a female relative or else financial gain because of some else's money, probably through a marriage or partnership.

Reversed Meaning:
Often this card in the reversed position indicates that you are keeping a deep secret that is literally poisoning you internally. Poorly placed, this card may suggest that you are abusive or suppressive. In a man's reading, it can reveal a negative connection with his mother, which has "poisoned" his relationships with women ever since. You may be hiding a secret love affair, secretly jealous of another, or else lost in the illusion of

beauty and the ideal woman in a hopeless attempt to escape hungering emptiness. This card may also indicate extreme confusion and trauma with regard to sexuality, to which you have responded with extremes: you could be a nymphomaniac or else a 45-year-old virgin.

8 of Cups
ABANDONED SUCCESS

Key Concepts:

- Not all is lost—it is not as hopeless as it seems
- The path of least resistance leads to loss
- Inaction as a result of feeling old and useless

Upright Meaning:
This is a situation of abandoned success: if only you will persevere, things will work out. Lethargy and lassitude are the paths of least resistance, but don't be fooled. You are missing or giving up too soon on an important opportunity. There may be hidden trouble at work, as well as things going on behind your back. This card encourages you that you are NOT too old to succeed.

Reversed Meaning:
You feel as though you have lost what's important and are "over the hill," wanting to give up and not seeing beyond the present apparent hopelessness of the situation. Perhaps you are overempathizing with someone else's loss, finding it difficult to refrain from helping and therefore losing your self-identity in the instinct to not "abandon" another. If well placed, this card reversed may indicate that you are beginning to separate from the external world and focus inward.

9 of Cups
INDULGENCE

Key Concepts:
- Celebration, intoxication, and excess
- Hidden addictions and temptations
- Suffering after overindulgence

Upright Meaning:
If the card is well placed, it indicates gladness and festivity; generally, intoxicating immersion in material happiness to the point of gluttony. If the card is poorly placed, there may be hidden alcoholism, drug problems, codependency, or seduction. Be wary of superfluous spending, gratuitous sex, getting fat, and the negative affects of too much celebration. If the card is very poorly placed, not everything may be as wonderful as it seems—watch out for ulterior motives.

Reversed Meaning:
If the card is well placed, you are seeking happiness and bliss—either through celebration and indulgence or else through spirituality and seclusion. If the card is poorly placed, you are easily deceived and exploited. There is a level of distraction as you throw yourself into enjoyable experiences to avoid confronting yourself.

10 of Cups
HAPPINESS

Key Concepts:
- Completion and happy endings
- Something hidden in what you thought you wanted
- Feeling trapped in a heaven of your own choosing

Upright Meaning:
The 10 of Cups brings happiness in relationships. You will find the community you seek. Your emotional ideals will be fulfilled, but watch out for losing yourself in the process. The 10 of Cups cautions us that when we are too focused on happiness, however, we lose the will to change: happiness lulls us into contented inaction and acceptance of the status quo, shielding our eyes from the facts of the evils and injustices of this world, for in order to remain happy ourselves, it is necessary to ignore the unhappiness of others. The panacea of our modern age is the lie of the pursuit of happiness as an end unto itself. Your ideals may have created a risky relationship or situation from which it will be difficult to break out, so watch out. If the card is very well placed, you may be called to an important spiritual quest but don't see it yet.

Reversed Meaning:
When well placed, this card suggests that you are a devoted, imaginative idealist who doesn't see the darker sides of existence. You are happy in your life and the community of people you love. If the card is poorly placed, you may want to escape the situation that you have created, for you are blinded by ideals to the reality of the situation. Perhaps you are dedicated to the pursuit of happiness to the exclusion of all else. Beware of enforcing your rigid view of how life "should" be on everyone around you.

THE SWORDS SUIT
the symbol

The final suit of the Minor Arcana is the transmissive Air element, represented by the Sword. To understand the logic behind the choice of this symbol, one has only to look at it: a sword is a phallus crafted for combat. Its sharp blade slices through the insubstantial air and penetrates to the heart of the matter, giving you the upper edge. Battles have been won or lost, agreements made or broken, by the strength of the Sword. The Swords suit rules those arenas that are antagonistic, sharp, penetrating, and interested in winning the upper edge—opposition, reason, the mind, and communication. Any matter decided by the Sword (or by opposition, reason, and communication, for that matter) by its very nature is impermanent: it takes constant vigilance to maintain a superior position. Is there perhaps a higher path that transcends the inherent transience of the Sword?

Ace of Swords
POWER OF AIR

Key Concepts:
- Powerful beginning in the realms of intellect, communications, and discord
- Use reason and intellect to confront the current situation
- Successful resolution of disagreement

Upright Meaning:
The Ace of Swords can often herald a new message, contact, or discussion. This card usually portends a powerful beginning in the realm of Air, involving intellect, discord, or communication. Sometimes this card announces a new relationship, but generally this card promises you a powerful position with regard to these matters, especially if you remain objective.

Reversed Meaning:
If the card is well placed, you possess the capacity to succeed in the endeavor(s) under consideration. If the card is poorly placed, you may be seeking a disagreement or communication, but there are obstacles that must first be acknowledged and faced. To know the obstacles, look to the surrounding cards. If the card is very poorly placed, you may be trying to prove that you are right or to justify your actions rather than confront the facts.

2 of Swords
HARMONY

Key Concepts:

- Peace temporarily restored
- Positive settlement of legal disputes and personal disagreements
- New partnerships or next level of commitment

Upright Meaning:
Peace will be restored, but the truce will not be permanent because the issues are not truly resolved. You will handle your opponents effectively and your relational problems will improve. There will be a positive settlement of any legal disputes. If the card is well placed and you do not have a partner, then a new partnership may be coming. If you do have a current partner, this card suggests that the relationship will reach a new level of contractual commitment.

Reversed Meaning:
You are seeking harmony, regardless of the costs to yourself or others. If the card is well placed, you have the common sense necessary to successfully handle your opponents. This card reversed may also suggest that you want a permanent commitment of some kind.

3 of Swords
SEPARATIONS

Key Concepts:
- Grief from separation or ending of a partnership
- Current relationships have a flawed foundation—time to renegotiate
- Loss of job, partnership, court case, or argument

Upright Meaning:
Loss and separations. Sorrow resulting from the loss of a partnership, a job, or a judgment. This card may signify a lost item or circumstance that will never be regained. This card can also herald the separation or ending of a relationship, either through breakup, divorce, or even physical death. The arrangements of prior agreements or partnerships need to be renegotiated: their structure has altered to such a degree that they are obsolete, so it is time either to let go of them or else create a new foundation. If poorly placed, this card may warn of serious illness. If it's well placed, these losses will ultimately benefit you.

Reversed Meaning:
Generally, this card reversed suggests either that you are afraid that your current partnership is ending, or else you want out of it your relationship badly. If the card is well placed, this desire is justified. If the card is poorly placed, your reasons for leaving (or not leaving) are inadequate—you may be promising more to your partner than can possibly be given, or else are unable to make the painful but necessary decisions that need to be made about your current partnership. Sometimes, if very well placed, this card suggests that you are willing to work hard and are determined to make a flawed partnership last.

4 of Swords
PARTNERSHIP

Key Concepts:

- Rest from current strife
- Success in all forms of partnerships
- The professionals you consult will provide excellent advice

Upright Meaning:
You will expand your life through interactions with others: you are entering a period of rest from stress in which the current problems will be resolved. There may be a like-minded, spiritually progressive soulmate relationship entering your life. Any professional consulted for assistance (from lawyer to marriage counselor) will bring success. You will succeed in helping opposing parties resolve their differences, as well as in negotiating a business deal to the benefit of all involved. If poorly placed, this card calls for you to meditate and contemplate on the issue before making a decision: there may be a tendency to jump into grand speculations without thoroughly weighing all sides.

Reversed Meaning:
If the card is poorly placed, you may be trying to satisfy all involved and therefore satisfying none. Perhaps you are looking for your soulmate or desire a new business partnership. If the card is well placed, you know that you are blessed in your partnership(s) and are benefiting financially, emotionally, and spiritually from them.

5 of Swords
LONGING

Key Concepts:

- Dreams become delusions as what seemed perfect turns rotten
- Betrayal in partnerships and loss of reputation
- Poor investments of a personal nature as well as a financial one

Upright Meaning:
You are caught in circumstances that were originally beautiful but have now turned ugly. Your dreams and ideals that should have been sweet have turned into nightmares: Relationship(s) have gone sour, there has been betrayal, there is poor public opinion, and activities that at first seemed important now seem a complete waste of time. Love may come into your life, but ultimately it won't work. If you are currently in a relationship, you are both living separate lives. If the card is very well placed, a current friendship may develop into romance, or else you may actually benefit from another's losses.

Reversed Meaning:
You feel defeated and hopeless because of your failure to accomplish your dreams. You are probably mourning or refusing to let go of a lost love. If currently involved with someone, you are emotionally distancing from your partner. Sometimes this card suggests that you may be seeking an open relationship or else have a romantic interest in a friend. If very well placed, this card can suggest that you don't think that your lover is "the One"—but you are mistaken, for this is the Real Thing. Often, people with this card reversed are projecting their own romantic notions and past history with women (especially their mothers) upon the other, failing to see their partner as he or she truly is.

6 of Swords
FRESH HORIZONS

Key Concepts:

- Be ready for good news
- Leaving a bad situation for a better one
- Change will bring increase and help you realize your dreams

Upright Meaning:

There's good news coming! This card encourages you that you are leaving an inferior situation for a superior one. There will be well-earned successes as well as good advice from friends. You will soon realize your dreams of travel, education, and philanthropy. Even if the card is poorly placed, you will ultimately benefit from a radical change.

Reversed Meaning:

You are actively seeking an innovative solution to the current situation. You are intelligent, impartial, honest, and open and may be a teacher or humanitarian. Even if poorly placed, this card portrays you in a positive light. You will find contentment if you make the change.

7 of Swords
FUTILITY

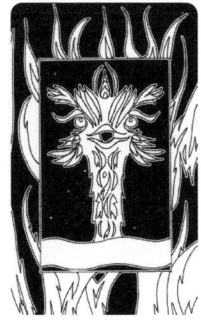

Key Concepts:
- Your good intentions and high ideals are insufficient
- Watch out for betrayal, public misinformation, liars, and thieves
- Any cause you feel drawn to right now is a lost cause

Upright Meaning:
Unstable effort arising from impossible dreams and good intentions. There may be broken promises, lies, or misinformation of the public. Watch for thievery: you may lose your resources by trusting the wrong person(s). Avoid joining losing causes. If you suspect betrayal or deceit, you are correct—the person can't be trusted. If you are expecting financial resources of some sort to arrive, you had better check up on it, because it is not what was promised.

Reversed Meaning:
If the card is well placed, you are a hopeless idealist who is easily fooled. Generally, you overthink and rationalize everything and are deceiving yourself. If the card is poorly placed, you are probably lying to yourself and others.

8 of Swords
SHORTSIGHTED

Key Concepts:

- Open your eyes—you're missing something important
- Be careful of snap judgments and groundless conjecture
- Misperception and misapprehension in all arenas
- Focusing upon appearance and image over substance and truth

Upright Meaning:

You are not seeing the situation(s) clearly right now. There will be unfounded speculation, misapplied ideas, and snap decisions based upon little substance. This card can even suggest that you need new glasses or a new hearing aid to help you perceive things more accurately. On the positive side, you might be a gifted actor, beautician, or some other profession adept at image and appearance. There may be a spiritual or religious teacher in your life who is much more concerned with how things look, rather than what things actually are.

Reversed Meaning:

You are blind to the truth but excellent at bluffing your way through life, having quick wits with little substance: It is important to you that others are impressed by your "knowledge." This card reversed may also suggest that your focus is upon image and appearance, such as fashion, movies, or beauty. Beware of becoming trapped by superficialities! If the card is poorly placed, you may be claiming a high status that you know you don't truly deserve.

9 of Swords
CRUELTY

Key Concepts:
- Nightmares, loud noises, arguments, and trouble sleeping
- Contract disputes and missing paperwork
- Rumors, gossip, and cruel intentions

Upright Meaning:
The 9 of Swords admonishes that when we believe ourselves to be victims of cruelty, we use this to justify our own cruel victimization of others. When our life seems a nightmare, we drag the nightmare around with us to disturb the lives of those around us. Watch out for suffering as a result of arguments—in the neighborhood, with brothers and sisters, or with an older woman. There will be loud noises and jarring energy surrounding you, resulting in troubled dreams and lack of rest or sleep. It is time to take decisive action to put an end to the discord, for neither party will ever see eye to eye as long as each is stuck in his or her own viewpoint. There may be a lack of proper credentials or paperwork, as well as possible fights over contracts. You might be heatedly questioned by a hostile source. Beware of malicious gossip or any news stories about yourself right now.

Reversed Meaning:
Generally, this card reveals you to be actively involved in heated arguments based upon a dogmatic viewpoint. If the card is poorly placed, you are being deliberately malicious and cruel in the process of attempting to win. If well placed, this card reversed indicates that you are concerned about the dissension surrounding you right now and want it to end: you wish to get to the bottom of the matter, cutting through the appearances. Stop justifying your bad behavior by claiming to be the victim.

10 of Swords
RUIN

Key Concepts:

- The current situation is ruined beyond repair
- Your reputation is in danger
- A critical communication is coming—watch for it

Upright Meaning:
The damage in the current situation(s) is already done. Words will cause (or have caused) ruin in some way: you should watch your reputation, for people are gossiping and backstabbing. If the card is very well placed, there may be a critical upcoming communication with brothers or sisters, many short trips, an important conversation, or some sort of image-based contact—possibly with the media.

Reversed Meaning:
Normally, this card reversed suggests that you are struggling with feelings of failure and ruin. If the card is poorly placed, you are intellectually arrogant, image driven, two faced, and superficial, and you damage others with your thoughtless words. This may be a message to avoid gossip, for your own cruel words will bring ruin. You may be seeking to move on to the next new and exciting experience rather than face the failure of the current situation.

PUTTING IT ALL TOGETHER THE CROSS TAROT SPREAD

At first it can be a bit overwhelming to know where to start when you are ready to move from playing with your Tarot deck to using it to answer your life's questions.

Key Concepts: This guide includes one comprehensive spread, the Cross Spread, as a starting point. The Cross Spread is a basic version of a popular method of laying out your Tarot cards that will address all aspects of a question. There are two basic types of readings: General Readings, in which you have no specific question(s) but simply want insights into your life at present, or else Specific Questions.

HOW TO PHRASE YOUR QUESTIONS

How you phrase your question will have a profound effect on the outcome of your Tarot reading. Ask a question that is too broad, requires the Tarot deck to make the decision for you, or is harmful to another person in some way, and you will find your answer confusing and quite impossible to clearly interpret.

A good place to begin for a General Reading is to simply ask, "What do the next three months (or six months, or a year) have in store for me?" Another effective way to phrase a General Reading might be this: "What do I need to know about my life right now?" or "What do I need to see more clearly in my life?"

To know how to phrase a Specific Question, let us consider some more-effective and less effective questions about the ever-popular subject of Love:

More-Effective Questions:

- What do I need to see that I am not seeing in my current relationship?
- What will happen in my relationship if I _____?
- Will I marry my current partner?
- Why have I been unsuccessful in finding a partner?
- What do I need to see in order to reach resolution with regard to the breakup of this relationship?

Less Effective Questions:

- Should I date (or marry) this person?
- Will I ever get married?
- How can I get him (or her) back?
- How can I get him (or her) to fall in love with me?
- How can I get revenge for what he (or she) did to me?

The first set of questions is effective because they are specific and seek further information to help you see more clearly and make appropriate choices. The second set of questions is less effective because they are either too general or else ask the cards to make the decision for you, some even exhibiting a desire to control or harm another. The more effective the question is, the more useful the answer will be.

READING YOUR CARDS

To begin a reading, thoroughly mix the deck until you instinctively feel that it is time to stop. Sometimes this takes only a few shuffles, but occasionally this can go on for a few minutes. What matters here is not how you mix the deck, but that you create a consistent ritual of mixing, so that every time you do a reading you create a sacred space by beginning the same way.

THE CROSS SPREAD

After mixing the deck, lay out ten cards in the form of a cross:

- **The Significator:** This represents you or the specific situation or problem of your question.
- **Crossing Card:** Reveals what is currently "crossing" (blocking, impeding, causing problems for) you or the situation.
- **What's Beneath:** What is really beneath your question? What are you focused on to the exclusion of all else?
- **What's Above:** What information is above you: obvious to others, but you are currently not seeing it?
- **What's Passing:** What has occurred recently in your life that has caused you to ask this question; what is passing away or will soon be gone from your life?
- **The Immediate Future:** What is in store for you in the immediate future, after you finish this Tarot reading?
- **Internal World:** What is the state of your internal world and how is it affecting your ability to effectively deal with your life or this problem? What are you bringing to the situation?
- **External World:** What is the truth of your external world? What external forces and events surround and influence you?
- **Distant Past:** What past issue or baggage do you still carry in the present that is blurring your ability to clearly perceive and act appropriately in the situation today?
- **The Final Outcome:** What is the ultimate outcome of this situation? What is the main message that you must understand in order to grow?

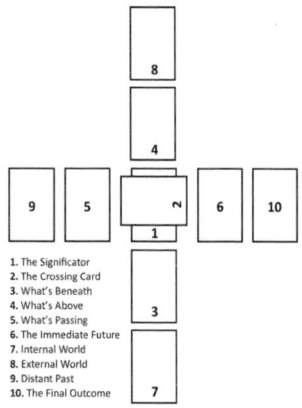

1. The Significator
2. The Crossing Card
3. What's Beneath
4. What's Above
5. What's Passing
6. The Immediate Future
7. Internal World
8. External World
9. Distant Past
10. The Final Outcome

YES OR NO QUESTIONS

Generally, it is not a good idea to make any decision when you are emotionally upset or physically weakened or when you know that you are not seeing clearly. If you don't have much time, you *can* get a quick yes or no to a simple question. Mix the cards and pull one card off the top of the deck. If the card is upright and positive, the answer is "yes." If the card is reversed and positive, the answer is "yes—but wait before acting." If the card is upright but its meaning is either negative or mixed, the answer is "no." If the card is reversed and either negative or mixed, a simple "yes" or "no" is not sufficient to answer the question: a more comprehensive spread is necessary.

Now, go color and play with your new Tarot deck!